The Tramway

(Networks Edition)

In 1971/5, the present publishers issued a two-volume history with the title *The Tramways of Kent*. It was written by a consortium of ten authors, who took as their joint *nom-de-plume* the name Invicta. The editor was Geoffrey E. Baddeley. These two books have been out of print for several years, and are still in demand.

In recent years, however, the same publishers have embarked on a series of more concise regional histories of British Tramways, using as texts the chapters of *Great British Tramway Networks* by W. H. Bett and J. C. Gillham. Although the tramways of Kent formed an incomplete coastal chain rather than a network, it is appropriate to re-issue *The Tramways of Kent* in a shortened form so that it may take its place in the regional series.

At the same time, we have extended the area covered to take in the three tramway towns in North West Kent (Bexley, Erith and Dartford) which although part of the London conurbation, were in Kent when they were served by tram. These sections are based on the same publisher's 1963 book *The Tramways of Woolwich and South East London* by 'Southeastern', again edited by Geoffrey Baddeley and long out of print. For a more recent account of tramways in Woolwich, the reader is referred to the London Tramways History Group's recent hardback *London County Council Tramways, Volume I, South London,* by E. R. Oakley.

The sequence in the present book is geographical, starting in North West Kent and following the Thames and Medway to Gravesend, Rochester, Chatham, Maidstone and Sheerness and the Channel coast to Herne Bay, Margate, Ramsgate, Dover, Folkestone, Sandgate and Hythe. We shall mention some proposed tramways that were authorised but not built, and others that failed to gain authorisation. These lines would have served in many cases to link those that were built. We shall also mention some cliff lifts and narrow gauge railways.

Bexley

In 1903, the Bexley Urban District Council opened a standard (4ft 8½in) gauge electric tram route from the Plumstead terminus of London's horse tramways, through Welling and Bexleyheath along the main London-Dover road to the Bexley/Dartford boundary just beyond Bexleyheath Market Place and the depot. There was a branch line running north from the Market Place to meet the proposed Erith tramways at Northumberland Heath. In 1908 the London County Council regauged and electrified the horse-tram route from Plumstead to Woolwich (Beresford Square) and Bexley skilfully negotiated through running to Beresford Square in exchange for a short piece of track that entered the LCC area at Plumstead. Paradoxically, the trams never served the old town of Bexley, although the power station was located there.

COVER PICTURE: Isle of Thanet 19 and one of the same company's buses at Margate Station in 1932. *(M. J. O'Connor*

The starting point of our journey is Beresford Square, Woolwich, terminus of the through service to Bexleyheath (and later to Dartford). This 1909 view shows a five-window Bexley Council tram alongside a three-window London County Council car for Abbey Wood. *(Commercial postcard*

During the 1914-18 war there was a tremendous increase in traffic in the area, because of the Arsenal and the munitions factories. Bexley hired a number of cars from the LCC, and this had to be increased in 1917, when the complete Dartford tram fleet was destroyed in a depot fire. After the war, Bexley arranged to purchase and retain twelve of these cars nominally for the use of Dartford and five for their own use. In fact, all 17 were used indiscriminately on the one long through route from Woolwich to Dartford and Horns Cross, together with Bexley's own 16 open-top cars.

Erith

The small industrial town of Erith on the south bank of the River Thames was served by a curiously shaped tram route which started just round the corner from the LCC terminus at Abbey Wood and ran via Belvedere to the centre of Erith, then south-west to meet the Bexley tramways at Northumberland Heath. There was also a short branch from Erith centre, due south to North End. Unfortunately, Erith Council were unable to persuade the LCC to take an interest in their system and connect the tracks at Abbey Wood, even though their line was laid with double track and clearances sufficient for bogie cars. (A connecting track for depot workings was put in by London Transport in 1933.) The North End route was not a success, even with one-man demi-cars, and closed in 1908. The long-sought-after through service from Erith to Woolwich materialised in 1935 as a trolleybus route.

The Bexley and Erith tracks were connected at Northumberland Heath, and after various arguments a through service was provided. Eventually Erith leased this section of Bexley track, and Erith cars worked Abbey Wood-Erith-Bexleyheath Market Place. As at Bexley, Erith tramways had to carry much extra traffic during the 1914-18 war and had to obtain some cars from other operators.

An opening-day scene on the Dartford Council tramways, 14 February 1906.
(Courtesy J. H. Meredith

Dartford

Crayford and Dartford were served by an electric tramway whose main line was a continuation along the Dover Road from the Bexleyheath boundary to Horns Cross, among the chalk quarries beyond Dartford. The line was physically connected with that of Bexley, and there were two short branches at Dartford, northwards to the railway station and the depot, and southward to the village of Wilmington. Although owned by Dartford Council, the system was constructed by and initially leased to J. G. White & Co. Ltd., who transferred the lease in 1909 to Balfour Beatty & Co. Ltd. There were twelve quite ordinary open top cars, in fact everything was ordinary about the Dartford Council Light Railways until August Bank Holiday 1917, when the depot was burned to the ground, with all the rolling stock and equipment. Crayford and Dartford with their war industries could not be left without a tram service, so Bexley bravely stepped in and lent them some cars.

Fortunately, the London County Council was willing to lend Bexley some cars at short notice, which it could spare because of wartime shortage of crews. After the war, Bexley purchased 17 of these Class B cars (twelve of them on behalf of Dartford Council). In April 1921, the lease having run out, Bexley and Dartford formed a Joint Committee to run their tramways from Bexleyheath depot. As well as the through service from Woolwich to Horns Cross there were still workmen's journeys to Dartford Station and a shuttle service with a single Bexley car from Dartford to Wilmington. The London Passenger Transport Board took over all public transport in the area on 1 July 1933, introducing some newer ex-LCC cars, but the North Kent trams were replaced in November 1935 by LPTB trolleybuses, which however did not go beyond Dartford.

River Hospitals

Dartford also had within its boundaries a horse tramway system of 4ft gauge, whose existence was probably unknown to most people, as it ran on land inaccessible to the public. It was constructed in 1897 by the Metropolitan Asylums Board to serve the isolation hospitals on the marshes to the north of Dartford town, and was not used until the smallpox epidemic of 1902, when four secondhand horse trams were acquired. These collected the patients from the paddle steamers of the River Ambulance service at Long Reach and took them to the Long Reach or Orchard Hospitals (which were hutted camps) or to the permanent hospital at Joyce Green, where there was a circular route and several branches. One branch ran to the main gate to collect coal and supplies from tradesmen, whose own vehicles could not enter the grounds during epidemics. Five purpose-built ambulance trams were acquired in 1905-09, each pulled by a single horse. From May 1925 the horses were replaced by Talbot motor ambulances, which had to keep on the tram track in front of each car. Regular operation ceased in October 1930, but there was occasional operation until 1936; the rails were mostly lifted in 1943.

Gravesend

Early in 1906 Dartford Council applied unsuccessfully for powers to extend the Horns Cross route for some two miles through an area of chalk quarries, cement works and paper mills to meet the Gravesend tramways at Swanscombe. These were the electric successors to the Gravesend, Rosherville and Northfleet Tramways Co. Ltd., whose 3ft 6in gauge horse trams ran for 1½ miles from 1883 between Gravesend and the "Leather Bottel" at Northfleet. An extension through Northfleet to Huggins College was authorised in 1884 and built in 1888-9 by the Series Electrical Traction Company to demonstrate their system of electric traction with underground conduit supply. These trials, with two Brush-built cars, lasted from March 1889 to November 1890, after which the entire line was horse-worked.

A contemporary engraving of the Series Electrical Traction Company's experimental conduit tramway of 1889 at Northfleet. The car is emerging from its depot alongside "Ye Olde Leather Bottel". On the left, a horse tram arrives from Gravesend.

(Illustrated London News

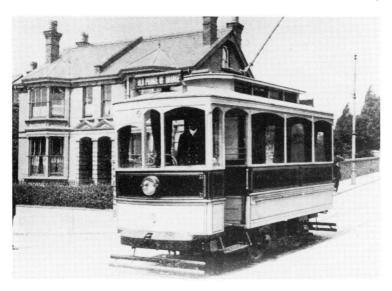

Four Kentish tramways tried using small one-man "demi-cars". The first two were Gravesend 9 and 10 of 1904 (as shown above). Erith Council bought two in 1906 (15 and 16) but resold one later to Dartford, and Maidstone Corporation bought a slightly larger one in 1909 (No. 18). *(TMS*

The Gravesend horse tramway was taken over in 1901 by The Gravesend and Northfleet Electric Tramways Limited, a member of the British Electric Traction group, who electrified the line and changed the gauge to standard 4ft 8½in to facilitate eventual through running with Dartford. Unfortunately, all such proposals were rigorously opposed by the South Eastern and Chatham Railways, and although the Gravesend line was extended to Swanscombe (Craylands Lane) the final link-up with Dartford was not built. For most of the day, the trams turned back at Swanscombe (George & Dragon), eventually with a motorbus connection to Horns Cross, but trams ran at peak hours to Craylands Lane to serve the cement works, which had an internal railway system worked partly by four former steam tram engines built in 1884 for Plymouth.

In addition to the main route, which ran through Northfleet on a high causeway between two large chalk pits, there was a branch line in Gravesend to the "Old Prince of Orange" and a loop line between Gravesend and Northfleet (Leather Bottel) via Pelham Road and the depot. The company started out with ten large bogie cars and ten four-wheelers, but the bogie cars proved too large and were passed on to other companies in the BET group, being replaced at Gravesend by further four-wheel cars including two one-man demi-cars and (in 1921) two single-deckers from Taunton. In the 1920s the company operated a number of feeder bus services, but in 1929 Maidstone & District buses replaced the trams. In 1933 these routes were taken over by London Transport's Country buses.

Military Road, Chatham.

The narrow gauge of 3ft 6in was adopted by the Chatham and District Light Railways on account of the narrow streets, especially in Rochester where the Chatham trams ran on tracks owned by Rochester Corporation. This scene is in the centre of Chatham. The fountain was later removed. *Commercial postcard, Balmoral Series*

Rochester and Chatham

The largest tramway system in this book, at almost 15 miles, was that which served the Medway towns of Rochester, Chatham and Gillingham. There were nine 3ft 6in gauge routes, with a complicated layout that included steep hills and narrow streets. The operator was the Chatham and District Light Railways Company (a subsidiary of British Thomson-Houston), though the tracks in Rochester were leased from Rochester Corporation. The fleet comprised about 50 green and cream open-top cars. The centre of the system was at Chatham Town Hall, and the outer termini were at Dockyard, Gillingham Strand, Gillingham Green, Rainham, Chatham Cemetery, Luton, Borstal, Frindsbury and Strood; the 1906 line to Rainham from Jezreels Corner (where there was a large folly) was mainly on roadside sleeper track. Powers were sought in 1903 for a line to Maidstone and for another in the direction of Gravesend, the company's stated objective being to take visitors to Charles Dickens' former home at Gads Hill, Higham, but neither line was built.

The Chatham company was taken over in 1929 by Maidstone and District Motor Services, and the trams were replaced by motor buses in September 1930. The buses retained the Chatham & District title and the light green livery (with light brown upper decks) until absorbed by Maidstone and District in 1955.

Maidstone

Maidstone, the County Town of Kent, stands on the River Medway south of Chatham and is a centre of the brewing industry. Like Chatham, it never had a horse tramway, but from July 1904 it enjoyed the benefits of a 3ft 6in gauge municipal electric tramway. One route ran from a stub in the High Street across Maidstone Bridge to Barming, another ran south to Loose, and the third was a short route serving paper mills at Tovil. There were seventeen open-top four-wheel cars, and in 1909 a demi-car was acquired to work the Tovil route; there was also a track-watering and snowplough car. All were painted in a light brown livery, known as "Golden Ochre" but which soon darkened to khaki. There were some municipal bus routes from 1924 onwards, and the trams were replaced by trolleybuses as early as 1928-30, but motor buses took over in 1967.

Sheerness

The small town of Sheerness, on the Isle of Sheppey, had a tramway system which was unusual in more than one respect. Its three short routes totalled only 2½ miles, radiating from the Clock Tower to the Pier, to Cheyney Rock, and to the level crossing at Sheerness East station on the Sheppey Light Railway, adjacent to the depot and power station. This windswept tramway system was owned by the British Electric Traction group, who had it equipped in 1903 by Siemens of Germany. Instead of having trolley poles, these cars had enormous bows, mounted on top of trolley masts on the upper deck; they had to be walked round at each end of the route. The overhead suspension was of Siemens German type with curved bowstring brackets, and depot access was by a turntable.

The twelve cars ordered were soon found to be more than sufficient, and four were quickly disposed of to another BET company. Another was altered for one-man operation on the Cheyney Rock branch. Traffic did not come up to expectations, and during the 1914 war the supply of spare parts from Germany dried up and there were troubles with the insulation of the bows. The tramway closed suddenly on 7 July 1917, the first electric tramway system in Great Britain to do so. The cars, less their bows, were sold to Darlington Corporation.

Herne Bay

There was only one genuine pier tramway in Kent, at Herne Bay, serving the Thames steamers. The first pier was built in 1832, and had rails on which a sail-driven car ran. This pier was replaced in 1873 by a new one. In 1898-9 this was extended to three quarters of a mile and provided with a 3ft 4½in gauge electric tramway with current supply through an off-centre slot conduit. The car was a Brush six-window single-decker on Peckham reversed maximum traction trucks. At first this car was used on its own, but in 1901 two cross-bench Bristol horse cars were acquired and converted to control-trailers. Soon afterwards one of them derailed and fell off the pier into the sea, with one fatality.

The Pier company sold out to Herne Bay Urban District Council in 1909. The tram ceased to run in 1914 and was succeeded by a petrol car in 1925 and a battery-electric car in 1934, which ran until 1939.

Herne Bay also figured in two ambitious applications for powers to build cross-country tramways. One, rejected by the Light Railway Commissioners in August 1901, was from Canterbury through Sturry and Herne Bay to Whitstable, the other (in 1902) was just from Canterbury to Herne Bay. The 1901 application failed by reason of narrow road widths, and no work was done on the other scheme.

Isle of Thanet

The most picturesque tramway in Kent was that of the Isle of Thanet Electric Tramways & Lighting Co. Ltd., which ran (partly along the sea front) from Margate through Broadstairs to Ramsgate. There was a cutoff inland past the depot at St.

From 1901 to 1937 the trams of the Isle of Thanet Electric Supply Co. offered a scenic open-top ride between Margate and Ramsgate. This view shows car No. 35 at Northdown Road. *(D. W. K. Jones*

Peters, with a private cross-country reservation between Northdown and St. Peters. On entering Ramsgate the line followed a steep and winding road down from the cliff top to the harbour, from where the line made a tour around the town to finish in the then SER station forecourt. An alternative route known as the Top Road served the inland part of Broadstairs.

Operations began in 1901 with 20 open-top four-wheeled and 20 open-top bogie cars, all built in America. Difficulties were soon experienced with the bogie cars, which could not easily be fitted with mechanical track brakes, and after a serious runaway all the bogie cars were shortened and mounted on four-wheel trucks. Two further accidents occurred in summer 1905, in one of which car 41 fell over the cliff at Ramsgate; fortunately no-one was killed. The fleet was rebuilt after the 1914-18 war, but was little altered in appearance. The company operated a profitable electric lighting business, and some feeder bus services. These were sold to the East Kent Road Car Company in 1937, and the trams were abandoned at the same time.

Meanwhile, summer 1936 saw the opening of the 2ft gauge Ramsgate Tunnel Railway, from Hereson Road to Ramsgate Harbour, running largely in a disused main line railway tunnel. The two four-car trains consisted of cross-bench coaches articulated to small mining-type locomotives with trolley poles. The tunnel served as an air raid shelter during the war, but the railway reopened in 1946 and ran until 1965. The tunnel had been disused since the main line was diverted in 1926.

The long gap between Ramsgate and Dover was to have been filled by what would have been the most ambitious tramway project ever launched in Britain. Announced in 1899, the Cinque Ports Light Railway would have comprised 67¾ (!) miles of 3ft 6in gauge electric tramway from Ramsgate Harbour through Sandwich, Deal, Dover, Folkestone, Hythe, Dymchurch, Romney to Lydd, then across Romney Marsh to Rye, Winchelsea and Hastings. Through running was envisaged from Margate to Bexhill, by agreement with the Isle of Thanet, Dover and Hastings

Dover on 6 September 1897 became the first town in Kent to have a municipal electric tramway, complete with American Providence-type lifeguards. *(Ray Warner*

tramways, but Dover Corporation were not in favour and the scheme collapsed in 1900. Part of it was revived in 1909 in the form of the Dover, St. Margaret's and Martin Mill Light Railway, but this did not materialise.

Dover

The seaport town of Dover, gateway to the Continent, had the earliest electric street tramway system in the south of England. It never enjoyed horse tramways, but its municipal electric system, comprising two routes, opened in 1897. The main route started near the Harbour Station and ran along the Docks, then turned inland through the town centre to Buckland, and there was a branch from near the Market Place along the Folkestone Road to Maxton. The main line was later extended, largely on private track, from Buckland depot to the village of River.

The original fleet of 16 trams consisted of short-canopy open-top cars, to which eleven standard type cars were added later. Dover tramways suffered from neglect and war damage between 1914 and 1918, with a serious accident in 1917, but instead of rebuilding the fleet or converting to trolleybuses, their manager went into the second-hand market and bought both complete cars and parts from which to re-create cars. Many of these had top covers, which were not really allowed on seaside narrow-gauge systems, but he kept quiet about that and got away with it. This fleet was painted in a bewildering array of different liveries, and many remained thus. The Dover trams were replaced by East Kent buses at the end of 1936.

Folkestone

The resort and port of Folkestone was large enough to justify having tramways, but the use of overhead wires was prohibited by the Earl of Radnor, Lord of the Manor and owner of much of the town. This caused the BTH and the BET to withdraw their respective schemes, but three other companies were interested and intended to use the side-conduit, Dolter surface contact and Kingland surface contact respectively.

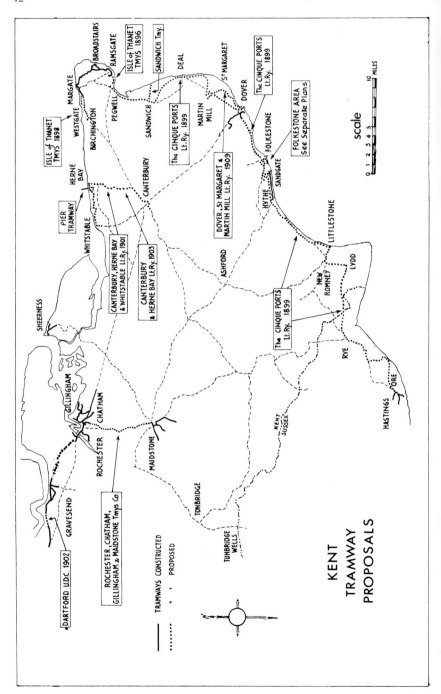

KENT
TRAMWAY
PROPOSALS

TRAMWAYS CONSTRUCTED
· · · · PROPOSED

scale

0 1 2 3 4 5   10
MILES

DARTFORD U.D.C. 1902

ROCHESTER, CHATHAM, GILLINGHAM & MAIDSTONE Tmys Co.

PIER TRAMWAY

CANTERBURY, HERNE BAY & WHITSTABLE L.I.Ry. 1901

CANTERBURY & HERNE BAY L.t.Ry. 1903

ISLE of THANET TMYS 1898

ISLE of THANET TMYS 1896

SANDWICH Tmy.

The CINQUE PORTS Lt.Ry. 1899

The CINQUE PORTS Lt.Ry. 1899

DOVER, St MARGARET & MARTIN MILL Lt.Ry. 1909

FOLKESTONE AREA See Separate Plans

The CINQUE PORTS Lt.Ry. 1899

BROADSTAIRS
RAMSGATE
MARGATE
WESTGATE
HERNE BAY
BIRCHINGTON
PEGWELL
DEAL
SANDWICH
St MARGARET
DOVER
MARTIN MILL
FOLKESTONE
SANDGATE
HYTHE
CANTERBURY
WHITSTABLE
SHEERNESS
GILLINGHAM
CHATHAM
ROCHESTER
MAIDSTONE
ASHFORD
LITTLESTONE
NEW ROMNEY
LYDD
RYE
ORE
HASTINGS
KENT SUSSEX
TONBRIDGE
TUNBRIDGE WELLS
GRAVESEND

Folkestone Corporation and Cheriton UDC favoured the Dolter system offered by the National Electric Construction Co. Ltd., but before construction could begin various defects in the Dolter system became evident elsewere, and the scheme collapsed.

The geography of Folkestone did however offer scope for funiculars (cliff lifts), of which there were four. Two were together near the Leas, one was near the Metropole Hotel, and one was at Sandgate Hill. Three were closed at various dates, but the oldest one, opened in 1885, is still working at the Leas and still operates on the water-counterbalance system. It is privately-owned, having been sold at auction by Folkestone UDC in 1987.

Sandgate and Hythe

From the foot of Sandgate Hill, a standard-gauge horse tramway ran for nearly four miles along the coast to Hythe. Part of it originated as a contractor's railway used in building the sea wall, after which it was left in place until completed and opened by the Folkestone, Sandgate and Hythe Tramways Co. Ltd. in 1891. It was absorbed by the South Eastern Railway in 1893, and the cars were overhauled as necessary at their works at Ashford. The line was nearly sold in 1906 to the National Electric Construction Co. Ltd. to form part of their proposed Folkestone system, but this did not proceed. It was closed during the 1914-18 war, but reopened with ex-Army mules in 1919, now running in the summer months only. It closed down in autumn 1921.

Other Lines

The earliest tramway scheme in East Kent was the Dover, Deal, Sandwich and Ramsgate Tramway Co. of 1871. This and its 1873 successor failed to proceed, but work did begin on a Margate-Ramsgate horse tramway in 1879, and one car was delivered, but the company was wound up in 1884. In 1895 there were proposals for a tramway from Sandwich to the beach, which would also have served the golf links. Eventually a 3ft 6½in gauge steam railway was built from a wharf on the River Stour to convey building materials for the Sandwich Bay Estate, but it was never used for passenger traffic.

The Chattenden and Upnor Light Railway, near Chatham, was a 2ft 6in gauge military railway from Upnor Pier to an ammunition depot at Lodge Hill, using steam, diesel and battery locomotives. At Lodge Hill it met the standard-gauge Chattenden Naval Tramway, which ran to Sharnal Street station on the Southern Railway's Isle of Grain branch. Standard gauge tramway track with grooved rail still exists in Chatham Historic Dockyard, and is used a few times a year to demonstrate steam cranes and a locomotive.

Another 2ft 6in gauge railway ran from Bowaters paper mill at Sittingbourne to Ridham Dock on the River Swale to carry wood-pulp from Scandinavia; part of it survives as the (preserved) Sittingbourne & Kemsley Light Railway.

On the 2ft gauge, the Ramsgate Tunnel Railway was not the sole example, for a diesel-operated line existed to serve Cobtree Manor Zoo near Maidstone. It closed in 1959 and the alignment is now used by the M20 motorway.

There were two 15 inch gauge public passenger railways in East Kent. One, now closed, was in Dreamland Amusement Park at Margate, but the other, the famous Romney, Hythe and Dymchurch Light Railway, is very much alive and is one of the best known of Britain's small gauge railways.

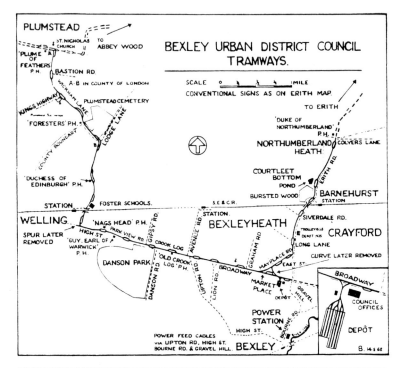

Bexleyheath Market Place about 1930, with an Erith Council open-top car on the left and two Bexley (ex-LCC) cars passing on the right. *(G. N. Southerden*

BEXLEY COUNCIL TRAMWAYS

Bexley 6 at Northumberland Heath, about 1906, looking north towards Erith. *(Courtesy J. H. Meredith*

Bexley 9 at Wilmington terminus in 1932. This shuttle service on Dartford UDC tracks required only one car. *(M. J. O'Connor*

Bexley 25 at Plumstead in 1929, about to turn right into Wickham Lane. The second car is an LCC Class E/1 for Abbey Wood. *(Science Museum, Whitcombe Collection*

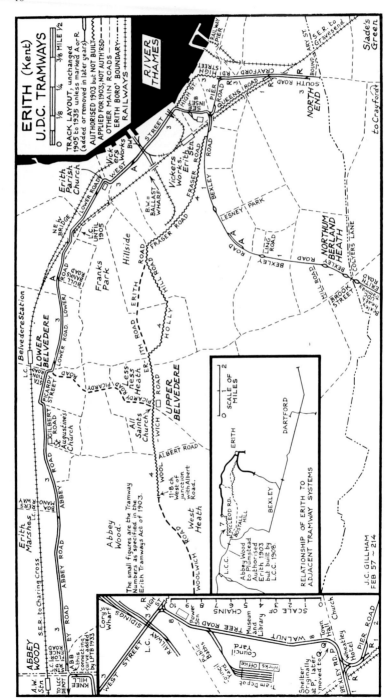

ERITH (Kent) U.D.C. TRAMWAYS

TRACK LAYOUT, unchanged
1905 to 1935 unless marked A or R.
(added or removed in later years)
AUTHORISED 1903 but NOT BUILT
APPLIED FOR 1903; NOT AUTH'RSD
OTHER MAIN ROADS
ERITH BORO' BOUNDARY
RAILWAYS

RIVER THAMES

RELATIONSHIP OF ERITH TO
ADJACENT TRAMWAY SYSTEMS

SCALE OF MILES

J.C. GILLHAM
FEB 57 ~ 214

The small figures are the Tramway
Numbers as specified in the
Erith Tramways Act of 1903.

SCALE OF CHAINS

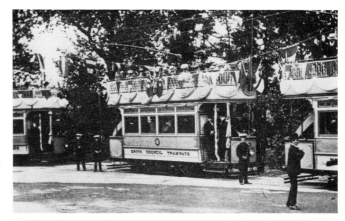

ERITH COUNCIL TRAMWAYS

The Erith tramways were ceremonially opened on 26 August 1905 with a parade of decorated cars. *(TMS*

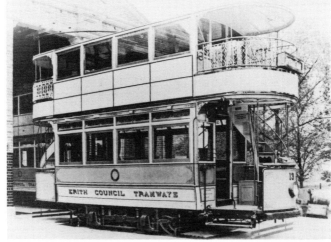

From 1905 to 1917 all the Erith trams were painted apple green and primrose yellow. Seven had top covers and seven had open top decks. *(Tramway and Railway World*

From 1918 to 1933 the Erith trams were in a more durable livery of dark red and ivory. No. 4 is shown here at the time of the LPTB take-over in July 1933 with the Erith title painted out.
(G. N. Southerden

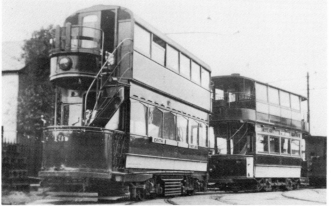

ERITH COUNCIL TRAMWAYS

Two former Erith cars (LPTB 19D and 10D) in Erith depot yard on 21 October 1933. No. 19 was bought from Hull in 1916.

(D. W. K. Jones

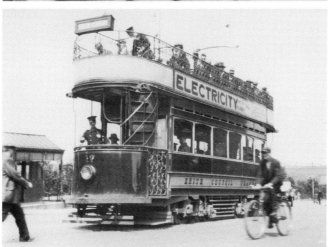

Erith 17 was one of four bogie cars (15-18) acquired from the London United Tramways. They were rebuilt in 1922 with top deck canopies and half-turn spiral stairs.

(Science Museum, Whitcombe Collection

London Transport 13D (formerly Erith 13) entering service from Abbey Wood depot in 1934, using the new curve linking the former Erith and LCC tramways.

(G. N. Southerden

19

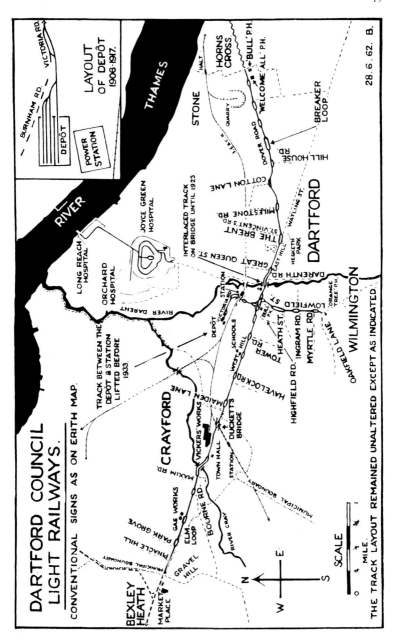

During a Fleet visit to the Lower Thames in August 1909, six Dartford Council trams were used to bring the sailors from Horns Cross to a parade in Dartford.

(Dartford Public Libraries

Four of Dartford Council's twelve Dick, Kerr cars at the Council's tram depot. On 7 August 1917 the depot and all the trams were destroyed by fire. Services were thereafter maintained by Bexley Council, using trams hired (and later purchased) from the London County Council.

(Dartford Public Libraries

TRAMS AT DARTFORD

B-Class car No. 34 at The Bull, Dartford, about 1919. The title "Dartford Council Tramways" is just visible on No. 34's rocker panel.
(Commercial postcard, Hawkes' Series

Ex-LCC B-Class car No. 30 at Horns Cross, the eastern extremity of the London tramway network. A 1½-mile gap separated this point from the Gravesend terminus at Swanscombe.
(G. N. Southerden

From October 1933 the Woolwich-Dartford service was worked wholly by ex-LCC Class M cars. No. 1689 is shown here at the top of West Hill, Dartford.
(B. Y. Williams

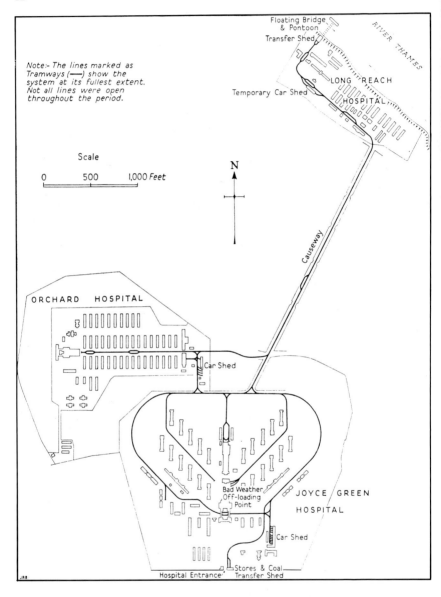

Note:- The lines marked as Tramways (——) show the system at its fullest extent. Not all lines were open throughout the period.

Floating Bridge & Pontoon
Transfer Shed
RIVER THAMES
LONG REACH
Temporary Car Shed
HOSPITAL

Scale

0   500   1,000 *Feet*

N

Causeway

ORCHARD HOSPITAL

Car Shed

Bad Weather Off-loading Point

JOYCE GREEN

HOSPITAL

Car Shed

Stores & Coal
Hospital Entrance   Transfer Shed

The 4ft gauge internal tramway system of the River Hospitals Tramway at Dartford was used to carry patients from the steamers of the River Ambulance Service to the wards of the isolation hospitals. The ambulance trams were horse-drawn until 1925 and towed by motor ambulances from May 1925 to October 1930. *(F. Merton Atkins*

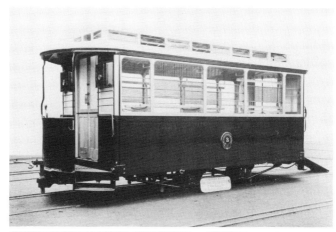

Ambulance tram No. 3 of the River Hospitals Tramway near Dartford, shown at the builder's works in Preston in 1909. The Metropolitan Asylums Board title appeared on a garter. *(U.E.C. Co.*

The five ambulance trams (Nos. 1 and 3-6) outside the depot at Joyce Green Hospital in the 1920s.
(Physician Superintendent, River Hospitals

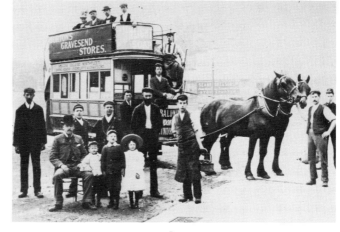

A horse car of the Gravesend, Rosherville and Northfleet Tramways Company outside the Northfleet depot.
(Courtesy the late Dr. Hugh Nicol

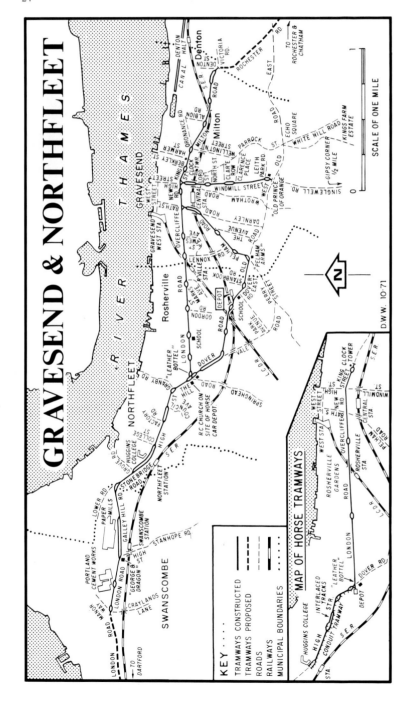

GRAVESEND & NORTHFLEET

MAP OF HORSE TRAMWAYS

KEY .....
TRAMWAYS CONSTRUCTED
TRAMWAYS PROPOSED
ROADS
RAILWAYS
MUNICIPAL BOUNDARIES

SCALE OF ONE MILE

D.W.W. 10-71

**GRAVESEND
AND
NORTHFLEET**

The only known photograph of the Series Electrical Traction experiment in 1889-90.
(Courtesy E. R. Oakley

A staff group at Gravesend depot in 1903 with one of the 1-10 Class bogie cars. These were later sold to Swansea, Jarrow and the South Metropolitan tramways and replaced by four-wheelers.
(The Tramway and Railway World

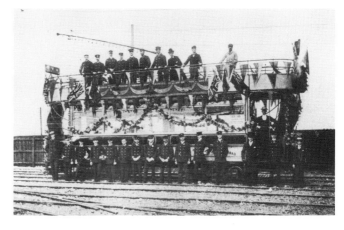

No. 12 decorated for the Gravesend Carnival in 1927. Nos. 11-20 of 1902 were later joined by three-window open top cars 1-6, which replaced the bogie cars.
(E. Fayne

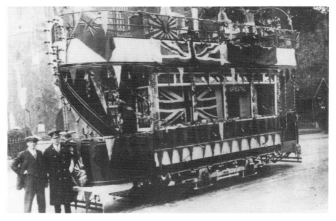

GRAVESEND AND NORTHFLEET

Gravesend 14 at Swanscombe terminus in the 1920s.
(Dr. Hugh Nicol

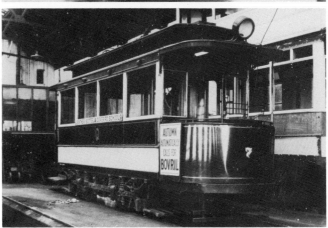

In 1921 the two Gravesend demi cars (illustrated on page 7) were replaced by two single - deckers bought from Taunton. The side route board reads 'Leather Bottel and Dover Road Schools'.
(Dr. Hugh Nicol

In 1924/5 six Gravesend trams (Nos. 15-20) were fitted with top covers made by Beadle Bros. of Dartford.
(E. G. P. Masterman

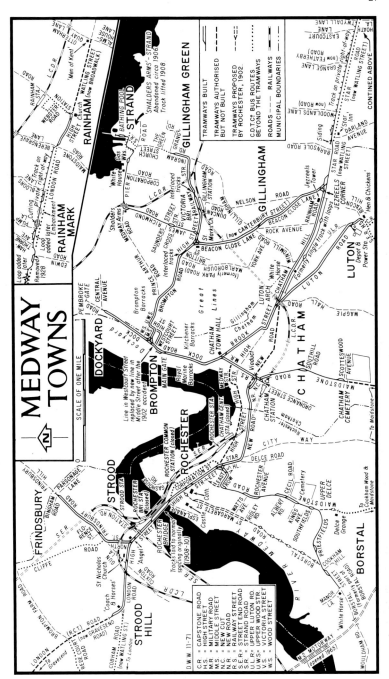

CHATHAM & DISTRICT

No. 8 in front of Chatham Town Hall in 1902. This was the centre of the 15-mile system. *(BTH*

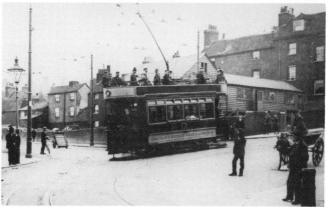

No. 7 at the foot of Westcourt St. in 1902, where soon afterwards No. 19 was involved in a serious runaway accident. *(BTH*

"Going to Dinner" is the caption to this 1904 picture of a line of trams at Chatham Dockyard.
(Gale & Polden

**CHATHAM
& DISTRICT**

**No. 51 at Frinds-
bury terminus in
1929.**
*(Science Museum,
Whitcombe
Collection*

**No. 8 on the
reserved sleeper
track of the
Rainham route
shortly before
closure on 30
September 1930.**
(A. W. Bates

**Chatham and Dist-
trict's Works Car
in Luton depot.**
(J. F. Higham

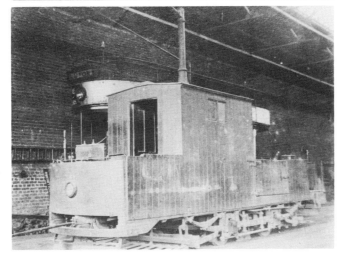

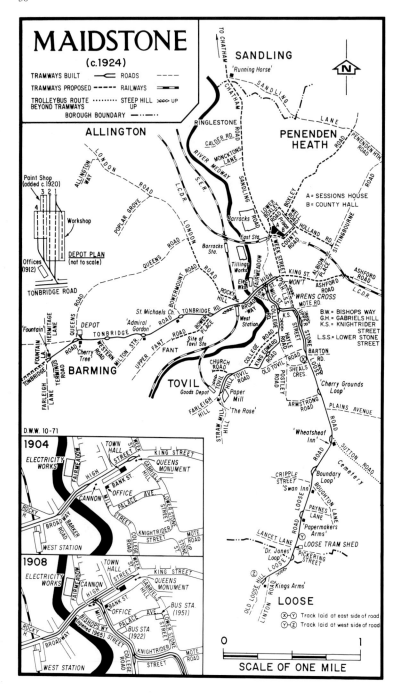

MAIDSTONE
(c.1924)

TRAMWAYS BUILT		ROADS
TRAMWAYS PROPOSED		RAILWAYS
TROLLEYBUS ROUTE BEYOND TRAMWAYS		STEEP HILL UP
	BOROUGH BOUNDARY	

SANDLING

'Running Horse'

TO CHATHAM

RINGLESTONE

CALDER RD.

MONCKTONS LANE

RIVER MEDWAY

CHATHAM ROAD

SANDLING ROAD

SANDLING LANE

PENENDEN HEATH

PENENDEN HTH ROAD

ALLINGTON

LONDON WAY

ALLINGTON WAY

POPLAR GROVE

ROAD

LONDON ROAD

QUEENS ROAD

BOWERMOUNT ROAD

L.C.D.R.

S.E.R.

Barracks Road

East Sta.

Barracks Sta.

Tillings Works

A = SESSIONS HOUSE
B = COUNTY HALL

LOWER BOXLEY ROAD
UNION ST
WELL ROAD
BOXLEY RD
COUNTY RD
WEST STREET

HOLLAND RD.

SITTINGBOURNE ROAD

ASHFORD ROAD

L.C.D.R.

KING ST.
ALBION PLACE

Paint Shop (added c.1920)
3 2 1
4
Workshop

Offices (1912)
DEPOT PLAN (not to scale)

TONBRIDGE ROAD

'Fountain'
HERMITAGE LANE

DEPOT

TONBRIDGE ROAD

WESTERN ROAD

MILTON STR.

UPPER FANT ROAD

'Admiral Gordon'

St. Michaels Ch.

TONBRIDGE RD.

BOWER PLACE

FANT

Site of Tovil Stn

CHURCH ROAD

TOVIL

Goods Depot

Paper Mill

'The Rose'

STRAW MILL HILL
TOVIL HILL
FARLEIGH HILL

TOVIL ROAD

OLD TOVIL ROAD

POSTLEY ROAD

SHEALS CRES.

BARTON RD.

'Cherry Grounds Loop'

ARMSTRONG ROAD

PLAINS AVENUE

'Wheatsheaf Inn'

SUTTON ROAD

ROCKY HILL
ELEC. WEST
HIGH ST.
MILL ST.
FAIRMEADOW
MONT
WRENS CROSS
MOTE RD.
BROADWAY
WEST STATION
COLLEGE ROAD
HAYLE ROAD
KING EDWARD RD.
STONE ST.
LOOSE ROAD

B.W.= BISHOPS WAY
G.H.= GABRIELS HILL
K.S.= KNIGHTRIDER STREET
L.S.S.= LOWER STONE STREET

ASHFORD ROAD

WRENS CROSS

MOTE RD.

BARMING

'Fountain'
TONBRIDGE
FARLEIGH LANE
TERMINUS
'Cherry Tree'
Queens Road

D.W.W. 10-71

CRIPPLE STREET

'Swan Inn'

Boundary Loop'

BOUGHTON LANE

PAYNES LANE

'Papermakers Arms'

LANCET LANE

LOOSE TRAM SHED

'Dr. Jones' Loop'

PICKERING STREET

Cemetery

LOOSE ROAD

LINTON ROAD

OLD LOOSE HILL

LOOSE

'Kings Arms'

X–Y Track laid at east side of road
Y–Z Track laid at west side of road

1904
ELECTRICITY WORKS

TOWN HALL

HIGH STREET
WEST STREET
MILL STREET
KING STREET
QUEENS MONUMENT

BANK ST.
OFFICE

CANNON

GABRIEL HILL
PALACE AVE.
LOWER STONE STREET
COLLEGE ROAD
KNIGHTRIDER STREET
MOTE ROAD

ROCKY H

BROADWAY

BARKER ROAD

WEST STATION

1908
ELECTRICITY WORKS

TOWN HALL

CANNON
HIGH
MILL STREET
WEST STREET
QUEENS MONUMENT
KING STREET

BANK ST.
OFFICE

BISHOPS WY (opened 1965)

BUS STA. (1951)

BUS STA. (1922)

GABRIEL HILL
PALACE AVE.
LOWER STONE STREET
COLLEGE ROAD
KNIGHTRIDER STREET
MOTE ROAD

ROCKY H

BROADWAY

WEST STATION

FAIRMEADOW

0 SCALE OF ONE MILE 1

MAIDSTONE

The opening pro-
cession of the
Maidstone Corp-
oration Tramways
in 1904, with cars
of series 1-6 en
route for Barming.
*(Commercial
postcard*

Maidstone 13 at
Loose terminus.
This route was
served by trams
from 1907 to
1930.
*(Courtesy
G. L. Gundry*

One Maidstone
car, thought to be
No. 14, was sold
in 1928 to Chat-
ham and District,
becoming Chat-
ham 52. It is
shown here at
Chatham's Luton
depot in August
1930.
(C. F. Klapper

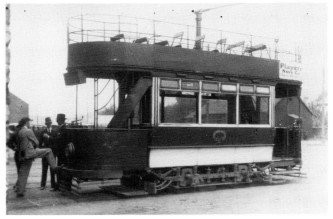

Maidstone 11 at Tovil terminus in 1929. Nos. 8 to 17 were a short version of the standard Dick, Kerr three-window cars used by many British tramways.
(Science Museum, Whitcombe Collection

Maidstone demi-car 18's body was rescued in 1971 after spending 43 years as a caravan at Winchelsea Beach. It is now at the Dover Pumping Station Transport Museum.
(J. H. Price

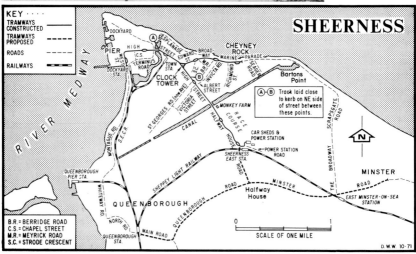

SHEERNESS

Uniquely in Britain the Sheerness tramways used Siemens bow collectors and bowstring bracket arms.

(Commercial postcard

Councils Schools, The Broadway, Sheerness-on-Sea

Two Sheerness trams at Moat Bridge on the Dockyard route. They ran for only 14 years, from 1903 to 1917.

(TMS

The centre of the Sheerness tramway system at the Clock Tower, with cars for Dockyard and Cheyney Rock.

(Valentines

The Crescent, Sheerness   Valentines Series

A passenger train on Bowaters' Sittingbourne Railway at Ridham Dock, with Bagnall 0-6-2T locomotive *Alpha*, 3 March 1957.
(J. H. Price

The three-car electric train of the Herne Bay Pier Company drew its power from a third rail in a conduit underneath the pier decking.
(Courtesy A. A. Jackson

A yellow 2-car train of the Ramsgate Tunnel Railway at Hereson Road terminus on 16 August 1959.
(J. H. Price

**ISLE OF
THANET**

**The sea front at
Margate about
1918, with cars 47
and 57 near the
Station.**
(Pamlin Prints

**A bogie car of
Series 21-40
a s c e n d i n g
Madeira Walk at
Ramsgate, about
1903.**
*(Commercial
postcard*

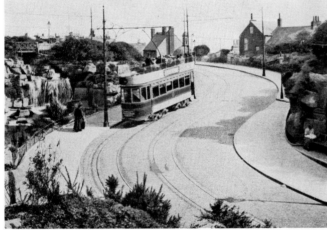

**A slightly later
view of Ramsgate
Harbour, showing
Nos. 8 and 21 on
the main line and
No. 45 on the spur
track.**
*(Commercial
postcard*

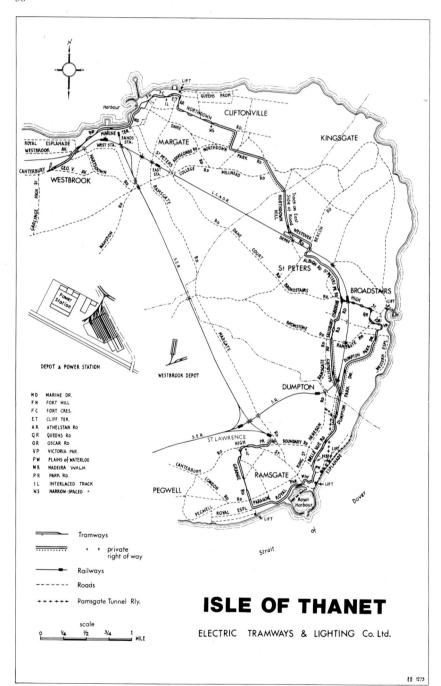

ISLE OF THANET

ELECTRIC TRAMWAYS & LIGHTING Co. Ltd.

DEPOT & POWER STATION

M D	MARINE DR.
F H	FORT HILL
F C	FORT CRES.
E T	CLIFF TER.
A R	ATHELSTAN RD
Q R	QUEENS RD
O R	OSCAR RD
V P	VICTORIA PAR.
P W	PLAINS of WATERLOO
M R	MADEIRA WALK
P R	PARK RD.
I L	INTERLACED TRACK
N S	NARROW-SPACED "

Tramways

" " private right of way

Railways

Roads

Ramsgate Tunnel Rly.

scale

0   ¼   ½   ¾   1
MILE

EB 1273

**ISLE OF
THANET**

Former bogie car
30 at Ramsgate in
final condition,
shortened and
placed on a four-
wheel truck.
(Dr. Hugh Nicol

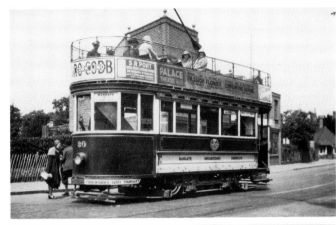

No. 36 on the
private track
between North-
down and the
depot, alongside
the unmade road.
(D. W. K. Jones

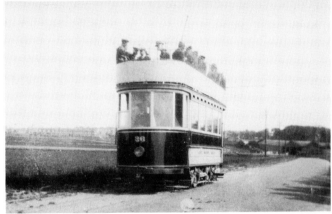

No. 45 after con-
version to a one-
man single-deck
car in the 1920s
for the inland "Top
Road" service
between Broad-
stairs High Street
and Ramsgate
Harbour.
(G. L. Gundry

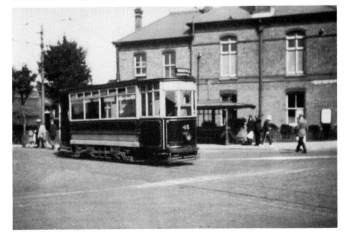

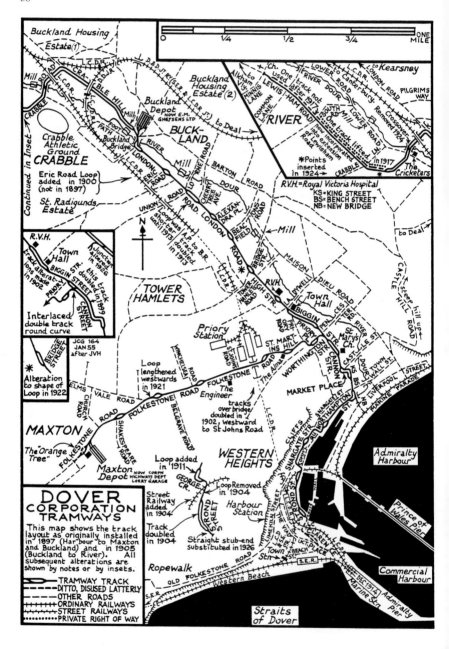

DOVER
CORPORATION
TRAMWAYS

This map shows the track layout as originally installed in 1897 (Harbour to Maxton and Buckland) and in 1905 (Buckland to River). All subsequent alterations are shown by notes or by insets.

TRAMWAY TRACK
DITTO, DISUSED LATTERLY
OTHER ROADS
ORDINARY RAILWAYS
STREET RAILWAYS
PRIVATE RIGHT OF WAY

DOVER

Dover Corporation Tramways opened in 1897 with ten open top cars (1-10) of which 8 and 10 were originally trailers.

(Cassiers Magazine

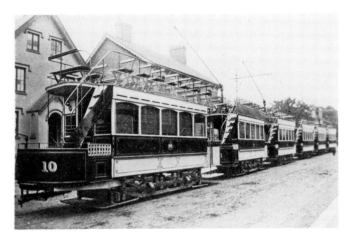

Dover 21 and two other new cars at the opening of the River extension on 2 October 1905.

(Courtesy W. J. Wyse

Dover 15 and 16 were built in the USA by J. G. Brill in 1898. No. 16 was given enclosed platforms in 1927.

(R. Elliott

DOVER'S SECONDHAND PURCHASES

Ex-Darlington 8 at Maxton terminus in 1926.
(Dr. Hugh Nicol

No. 3 (ex-West Hartlepool) on the River route in 1934. The second track had been lifted during the 1914-18 war.
(G. N. Southerden

No. 14 at Buckland Bridge. This car was bought by Dover in 1928 from the Birmingham & Midland Tramways.
(Dr. Hugh Nicol

Dover Corporation 27 passing a Southern Railway P-type tank engine in Strond Street,
July, 1934. *(G. N. Southerden*

Dover tram 22 (ex Birmingham Corporation) passing train ferry s.s. *Shepperton Ferry,*
laid up in Wellington Dock, Dover, early in 1936. This photograph appeared as the
frontispiece of the 1984 Jersey Artists' book *Night Ferry* by George Behrend and Gary
Buchanan. *(Fox Photos*

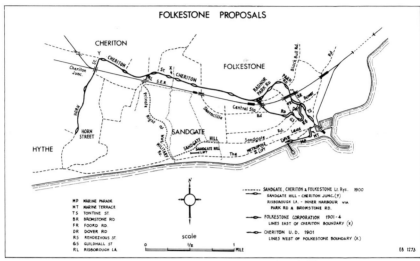

FOLKESTONE PROPOSALS

Folkestone's cliff lifts on 22 July 1972. The 1885 lift on the right is still in use, but the 1890 lift had ceased operation.
(J. H. Price

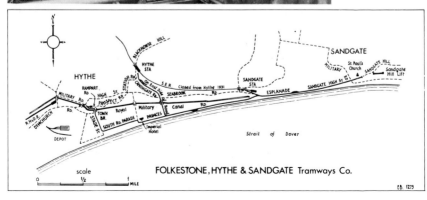

FOLKESTONE, HYTHE & SANDGATE Tramways Co.

**SANDGATE
AND HYTHE**

**Mule-powered
cross-bench car
No. 1 at Seabrook,
about 1920.**
(TMS

**Winter saloon No.
3 was built at
Ashford railway
works in 1892.**
(E. Harrison

**Open toastrack
No. 5 standing
outside the Hotel
Imperial at Hythe.**
(TMS

Tramcar Fleet Lists

All cars were four-wheel double-deck unless otherwise stated.

Seating figures shown thus: 22/34 are for lower and upper decks respectively.

The opening dates shown are the first day of regular public service.

The closing dates shown are the last full day of public service.

The fleet lists are arranged in the same geographical order as the main text.

Bexley Urban District Council Tramways

5.10 miles, 4ft 8½in gauge, opened 3 October 1903 by Bexley UDC, operated by Bexley Council Tramways and Dartford Light Railways Joint Committee from 1921 and by LPTB from 1 July 1933, closed 23 November 1935. Livery: maroon and cream, later chocolate and cream.

Car Numbers	Type (as built)	Year Built	Builder	Seats	Truck	Motors	Controllers
1-12	Open top	1903	ER&TCW	22/30	Brush A (note a)	DK 25A 2 x 25 hp	DK DB1 Form B (note b)
13-16	Open top	1904	ER&TCW	22/30	Brush A (note a)	DK 25A 2 x 25 hp	DK DB1 Form C (note b)
17-33 (note c)	Enclosed top	(bought 1918-20)	ER&TCW	22/38	Brill 21E	DK 25A 2 x 25 hp	DK DB1 Form D
34-39 (note d)	Enclosed top	(on hire 1918/20)	ER&TCW	22/38	Brill 21E	DK 25A 2 x 25 hp	DK DB1 Form D

Notes
(a) Nos 1-8 and 10-16 retrucked 1914 with Peckham Pendulum P22 type; No 9 retrucked 1918 with Brill 21E type.
(b) Three cars (including 14 and 16) received DK DB1 K3 controllers in 1914.
(c) Purchased 1918-20 from LCC Tramways (Class B), LCC numbers 109, 111, 112, 123, 128, 130, 139, 140, 151, 157, 167, 178, 180, 184, 187, 196, 201. Renumbering order not known, except that LCC 128 and 187 became Bexley 22 and 18. Previously on hire from LCC.
(d) Numbers allocated in theory to six cars hired from LCC in 1918-20 but not purchased, LCC numbers 101, 120, 131, 133, 169, 194. The only car known to have carried its Bexley number was 34 (possibly also 35).

After the formation of the LPTB on 1 July 1933, the Bexley cars were given a suffix of C to their numbers, but most were soon replaced by ex-LCC Class M cars (1453, 1468, 1677-1714, 1716-20, 1724/5). The Bexley trams were replaced by LPTB trolleybuses (Service 696), which ran from 24 November 1935 to 3 March 1959.

Dartford Urban District Council Light Railway

6.55 miles, 4ft 8½in gauge, opened 14 February 1906. Leased to J. G. White & Co. 1906-9 and to Balfour Beatty & Co. 1909-17. Operated 1917-21 by Bexley UDC, on behalf of Balfour Beatty, and from 1921 by a Joint Committee. For further details see entry for Bexley. Livery: (to 1917) maroon and cream or primrose.

Car Numbers	Type (as built)	Year Built	Builder	Seats	Truck	Motors	Controllers
1-12	Open top	1905	UEC	22/32	Brill 21E	DK 25B 2 x 25 hp	DK DB1 Form C
13	Single deck demi-car	(bought 1915)	Milnes Voss	20	M&G	Westinghouse 2 x 27 hp	Raworth

Car 13 was built in 1906 for Erith UDC (Erith No 15).

The entire Dartford tram fleet and depot was destroyed by fire on 7 August 1917. For subsequent operation see under Bexley (above).

River Hospitals Tramway, Dartford

3.40 track miles, 4ft 0in gauge, opened 27 February 1902, horse traction (motor haulage from May 1925), regular service ceased October 1930, occasional operation to 1936. Livery: ambulance trams navy blue and white, secondhand cars red. All cars single deck.

Car Numbers	Type	Year Built	Builder	Seats/berths	Truck
1	Large ambulance tram	1905	ER&TCW	10 berths	trunnions
3, 4	Large ambulance trams	1909	UEC	10 berths	trunnions
5, 6	Small ambulance trams	1909	UEC	2 seats/4 berths	trunnions

From 1902 to 1905 operation was by four secondhand London horse trams (5-8), for which the withdrawal dates were 5, 6 1906, 7 1931, 8 1925. There were also six 1904 Dick Kerr coal trolleys.
Four steam tram trailers had been purchased in 1902 (two each from Burnley and Huddersfield) but were not regauged or used.

Erith Urban District Council Tramways

4.70 miles, 4ft 8½in gauge, opened 26 August 1905, absorbed by LPTB 1 July 1933, closed 9 November 1935.
Livery: apple green and primrose, later dark red and ivory.

Car Numbers	Type (as built)	Year Built	Builder	Seats	Truck(s)	Motors	Controllers
1-6, 9	Open top	1905	Brush	22/30	M&G 21EM	Westinghouse 49B 2 x 30 hp	Westinghouse 90M
7, 8, 10-14	Balcony	1905	Brush	22/26	M & G 21EM	Westinghouse 49B 2 x 30 hp	Westinghouse 90M
15, 16 (note a)	Single deck demi car	1906	Milnes Voss	20	M&G Special	Westinghouse 2 x 27 hp	Westinghouse Raworth
15, 16 (II) 17, 18 (note b)	Open top bogie	(Bought 1919)	Milnes	30/44 (note b)	Brill 22E bogies	Westinghouse 2 x 30 hp	Westinghouse 90
19 (note c)	Balcony bogie	(bought 1916)	Milnes	30/46	Brill 22E bogies	DK 9A 2 x 40 hp	Westinghouse 90
20	Water car/ sweeper	1905	M&G	—	M&G	Westinghouse	Westinghouse 90

Notes
(a)   Demi-cars 15 and 16 were sold in 1915 to Dartford (13) and Doncaster (37) respectively.
(b)   Hired from 1915 from London United Tramways (LUT 187, 192, 221, 252). Original seating 30/39. Built 1902.
(c)   Built 1900 for City of Hull Tramways. Top-covered at Hull 1909.
After the formation of the LPTB on 1 July 1933, the Erith trams were given a suffix D to their numbers, and some were replaced by ex-LCC Class M cars.
The Erith trams were replaced by LPTB trolleybuses (698), which ran from 10 November 1935 to 3 March 1959.

Gravesend, Rosherville and Northfleet Tramways Co. Ltd.

2.19 miles, 3ft 6in gauge, horse traction, opened 15 June 1883, closed for electrification 30 June 1901.
Original fleet was five single deck cars, replaced by four double deck cars from 1898.
A short section of line at Northfleet was operated electrically from April 1889 to November 1890 on the Series conduit system, for experimental purposes.

Gravesend and Northfleet Electric Tramways

6.47 miles, 4ft 8½in gauge, opened 2 August 1902, closed 28 February 1929. Livery: maroon and cream, later cherry red and ivory.

Car Numbers	Type (as built)	Year Built	Builder	Seats	Truck	Motors	Controllers
1-10 (note a)	Open top bogie	1902	ER&TCW	32/36	Brill 22E bogies	DK 35A 2 x 35 hp	DK DB1 Form B
11-20 (note b)	Open top	1902	ER&TCW	22/36	Brill 21E	DK 33N 2 x 25 hp	DK DB1 Form B
1-4 (II)	Open top	1907	Brush	22/36	Brush AA	Brush 2 x 25 hp	Brush
5, 6 (II) (note c)	Open top	(bought 1909)	Brush	20/33	Brush AA	Brush 1002 2 x 35 hp	Brush HD2
7, 8 (II) (note d)	Single deck	(bought 1921)	Brush	24	Brush AA	Brush 1002D 2 x 20 hp	Brush
9, 10 (II)	Single deck demi-car	1904	Brush	22	Brush	Brush 1002A 2 x 27 hp	Raworth

Notes
(a)   The bogie cars were sold four to Swansea in 1904, four to South Metropolitan in 1906, two to Jarrow 1909 (probably 7-10 to Swansea, 1-4 to SMET, 5-6 to Jarrow).
(b)   Nos 15-20 received balcony top covers by Beadle Bros. in 1924/5.
(c)   Built 1906 for Jarrow and District Tramways (Nos. 5 and 6).
(d)   Built 1905 for Taunton Tramways. No. 7 converted at Gravesend to one-man car.

Sheerness and District Electrical Power and Traction Co. Ltd.

2.47 miles, 3ft 6in gauge, opened 9 April 1903, closed 7 July 1917. Livery: chocolate and cream.

Car Numbers	Type (as built)	Year Built	Builder	Seats	Truck	Motors	Controllers
1-8	Open top	1903	Brush	22/28	Brush A	Brush 1000A 2 x 25 hp	Brush HD2

Four additional cars of the same type were delivered to Sheerness but resold later in 1903 to the City of Birmingham Tramways Co. (CBT 189-192).
The eight cars were sold in 1917 to Darlington Corporation Light Railways.

Chatham and District Light Railways Company.

14.98 miles, 3ft 6in gauge, opened 17 June 1902, closed 30 September 1930. Livery: grass green (later light green) and ivory. 4.28 miles were owned by Rochester Corporation and 10.70 miles by the CDLR Co.

Car Numbers	Type (as built)	Year Built	Builder	Seats	Truck	Motors	Controllers
1-25 (note a)	Open top	1901	Milnes	24/26	Brill 21E	GE 58-6T 2 x 28 hp (b)	BTH B18
26-35	Open top	1902	Brush	22/26	Brush A	GE 58-6T 2 x 28 hp	BTH B18
36	Open top	1903	Milnes	24/26	Brill 21E	GE 58-6T 2 x 28 hp	BTH B18
37-41	Open top	1905	Brush	22/26	Brush AA	GE 58-6T 2 x 28 hp	BTH B18
42-46	Open top	1907	Brush	22/26	Brush AA	GE 58-6T 2 x 28 hp	BTH B18
47-48	Open top	1912	Brush	22/26	Brush AA	GE 58-6T 2 x 28 hp	BTH B18
49-51 (note c)	Open top	1914	UEC	24/26	Brill 21E	GE 58-6T 2 x 28 hp	BTH B49
52 (note d)	Open top	(bought 1928)	UEC	18/22	Brill 21E	DK 25B 2 x 25 hp	(BTH B18 at Chatham)

Notes
(a) No 19 destroyed in an accident, October 1902; truck and equipment used 1903 to build a works car with a Mountain & Gibson water tank. The rebuilt body of No. 19 may have become Car No. 36.
(b) Car No 8 received GE 249 37 hp motors in 1916.
(c) Five additional lower saloons at DK works in 1919 were completed for Stockport (61-5).
(d) Built 1907 for Maidstone Corporation as Maidstone 14.

Maidstone Corporation Light Railway

5.25 miles, 3ft 6in gauge, opened 14 July 1904, closed 11 February 1930. Livery: golden ochre and off-white.

Car Numbers	Type (as built)	Year Built	Builder	Seats	Truck	Motors	Controllers
1-6	Open top	1904	ER&TCW	22/26	Brill 21E	DK 25B 2 x 25 hp	DK DB1 Form C
7	Open top	1905	ER&TCW	22/26	Brill 21E	DK 25B 2 x 25 hp	DK DB1 Form C
8-17	Open top	1907	UEC	18/22	Brill 21E	DK 25B 2 x 25 hp	DK DB1 Form C
18	Single deck demi-car	1909	UEC	20	M&G 21EM	Westinghouse	Westinghouse TI/R (Raworth)
Works car	Water car/ sweeper	1908	M&G	—	M&G rigid frame	DK8A 2 x 37 hp	DK DB1 Form C

Car 14 was sold in 1928 to Chatham (Chatham No 52).
Three cars in series 1-17 ran for some years with Raworth regenerative equipment.
The trams were replaced by trolleybuses, which ran from 1 May 1928 to 15 April 1967.

Herne Bay Pier Co. Ltd.

0.65 miles, 3ft 4½in gauge, conduit current collection, opened 1 April 1899, closed 3 November 1939.

Motor car No. 1, 28-seat single deck saloon by Brush on Peckham Cantilever reversed maximum traction bogies with two GE 60 25 hp motors, withdrawn 1914. Service resumed 1925 with petrol-electric railcar (battery car from 1934). Control trailers 2 and 3, single deck 30-seat cross bench cars purchased from Bristol Tramways in 1901, fitted at Herne Bay with GE K10 controllers, withdrawn 1914. Livery not known.

Ramsgate Tunnel Railway

0.75 miles, 2ft gauge, opened 31 July 1936, closed 26 September 1965. Livery: 4 cars red, 4 cars yellow. Both trains built and equipped by EE. Each train: two motor cars and two control trailers, total seating 102.

Seven cars sold after closure to Hollycombe Woodland Garden Rly and the Hampshire Narrow Gauge Railway.

Cliff Railways	Year built	Length	Cars & tracks	Track Gauge	System	Closed
Broadstairs	1910	100ft	one	5ft 3in	electric	open
Folkestone (Leas) I	1885	164ft	two	5ft 10in	hydraulic	open
Folkestone (Leas) II	1890	155ft	two	5ft 0in	hydraulic	open
Folkestone (Metropole)	1904	96ft	two	5ft 6in	hydraulic	1940
Margate (Cliftonville)	1913	69ft	one	5ft 0in	electric	open
Sandgate Hill	1893	670ft	two	5ft 6in	hydraulic	1918

Isle of Thanet Electric Supply Co. Ltd. (see text for earlier title)

10.84 miles, 3ft 6in gauge, opened 4 April 1901, closed 24 March 1937. Livery: maroon and cream, later crimson and ivory.

Car Numbers	Type (as built)	Year Built	Builder	Seats	Truck	Motors	Controllers
1-20	Open top	1900	St. Louis	26/29	St. Louis cast frame (note a)	GE 58-6T 2 x 28 hp	BTH B18
21-40	Open top bogie (note b)	1900	St. Louis	30/38 (note b)	St. Louis 13 bogies (note b)	GE 58-6T 2 x 28 hp	BTH B18
41-50	Open top (note c)	1901	Milnes	24/28	Brill 21E	GE 58-6T 2 x 28 hp	BTH B18
51-60	Open top	1903	BEC	24/26	Brill 21E	GE 58-6T 2 x 28 hp	BTH B18
61	Works car	1903?	Own works	—	Brush AA	GE 58-6T 2 x 28 hp	BTH B18

Notes
(a) Retrucked from 1920s on Brill 21E or Peckham P22 trucks.
(b) Shortened in 1904 to seat 24/30 (?) and remounted some on Brush AA and others on Brill 21E trucks.
(c) Nos 42 and 45 later converted to single deck one-man cars. (42 kept its upper deck).
There were truck changes additional to those listed above.

Dover Corporation Tramways

4.29 miles, 3ft 6in gauge, opened 6 September 1897, closed 31 December 1936. Livery: green and ivory, later dark red and ivory (ex-Birmingham Corporation cars blue and cream).

Car Numbers	Type (as built)	Year Built	Builder	Seats	Truck	Motors	Controllers
1-10	Open top note a)	1897	Brush	20/24	Peckham Cantilever	GE 800-6T 2 x 20 hp	GE K2
11-14	Open top	1898	Milnes	20/24	Peckham Cantilever	GE 800-6T 2 x 20 hp	GE K2
15-16	Open top	1898	Brill	20/24	Brill 21E	Walker 33N 2 x 25 hp	Walker S/7
17	Open top	1902	ER&TCW	22/26	Brill 21E	DK 33N 2 x 25 hp	DK S/7
18-21	Open top	1905	ER&TCW	22/26	Brill 21E	DK 33N 2 x 25 hp	DK S/7
22-24	Open top	1912	Brush	22/26	Brill 21E	GE 58-6T 2 x 28 hp	GE K10D
25-27	Open top (note c)	1920	EE	22/26	Preston 21E	DK 30B 2 x 40 hp	EE DB1 K3
1-5 (II) (note d)	Open top	(bought 1927)	UEC	23/35	Preston Flexible	DK 13A 2 x 40 hp	DK DB1 K3
8, 9 (II) (note e)	Balcony	(bought 1926)	UEC	22/34	Preston Flexible	Siemens	Siemens (DK DBI K3 at Dover)
11, 12 (II) (note f)	Balcony	(bought 1928)	B&MTJC	22/26	Brush ?	GE 249A 2 x 37 hp	BTH B18
6, 7, 10, 14, 17 (II) (note g)	Balcony	(bought 1930)	Brush, rebuilt by B&MTJC	22/26	B&MTJC	GE 249A 2 x 37 hp	BTH B18
19-22 (II) (note h)	Balcony (note h)	(bought 1933)	UEC	22/27	Brill 21E	DK 25B 2 x 25 hp	DK DE1 Form G
Water car	track cleaner	1899	DK Kilmarnock?	—	Brill 21E?	Walker 33N	Walker S/1

Notes
(a) Cars 8 and 10 ran as trailers until 1898.
(b) Nos 13, 15, 16 rebuilt 1926/7 with extended canopies and additional top deck seats, EE K3B controllers and ex-Sheffield GE 58 motors.
(c) Nos 25-27 were fitted with ex B&MTJC top covers in 1928.
(d) Built for West Hartlepool Corporation in 1913 (West Hartlepool 1-5).
(e) Built for Darlington Corporation in 1913 (Darlington 17, 16).
(f) Built by Birmingham and Midland Tramways 1915 (Birmingham and Midland 15, 17).
(g) Built for Birmingham and Midland Tramways 1904 (14 at Tividale Works in 1915).
(h) Built 1905 for Birmingham Corporation Tramways. No 22 reconverted to open top at Dover. Two cars (probably 19 and 20) were placed on Dover's own Brill 21E trucks with DK 33N motors and controllers.

Folkestone, Hythe and Sandgate Tramway

3.36 miles, 4ft 8½in gauge, horse traction, opened 18 May 1891, absorbed by South Eastern Railway 1893, service suspended 7 August 1914 to May 1919, closed 30 September 1921. Livery: SER lake.

Car Numbers	Type	Year Built	Builder	Seats
1	Cross-bench single deck	1891	Milnes	40
2	Single deck open toastrack (roof added c. 1897)	1891	Milnes	40
3	Single deck winter saloon	1892	SER, Ashford	24?
4	Single deck cross-bench	1892	SER, Ashford	40
5	Single deck open toastrack	1897	SER, Ashford	45

Key to Abbreviations and Manufacturers

Brill	—	The J. G. Brill Company, Philadelphia, USA.
BEC	—	The British Electric Car Co Ltd, Trafford Park, Manchester.
BET	—	The British Electric Traction Co Limited.
B&MTJC	—	Birmingham & Midland Tramways Joint Committee, Tividale Works.
Bristol	—	The Bristol Wagon & Carriage Works Ltd, Lawrence Hill, Bristol.
Brush	—	The Brush Electrical Engineering Co Ltd, Loughborough.
BTH	—	British Thomson-Houston Co Ltd, Rugby.
DK	—	Dick, Kerr & Co Ltd, Preston.
Dolter	—	Dolter Electric Traction Limited, London E.C.
EE	—	The English Electric Co Ltd, Preston.
ER&TCW	—	The Electric Railway & Tramway Carriage Works Ltd, Preston.
GE	—	The General Electric Company, Schenectady, USA.
LCC	—	London County Council.
LPTB	—	London Passenger Transport Board.
Milnes Voss	—	G. C. Milnes, Voss & Co. Ltd., Birkenhead.
Milnes	—	Geo. F. Milnes & Co Ltd, Birkenhead and Hadley, Shropshire.
M & G	—	Mountain & Gibson Ltd, Bury, Lancashire.
Peckham	—	Trucks built by or for the Peckham Truck & Engineering Co Ltd.
Raworth	—	Raworth Traction Patents Ltd.
St. Louis	—	St. Louis Car Company, St. Louis (Mo.), USA.
Siemens	—	Siemens Brothers Dynamo Works.
SER	—	South Eastern Railway (Ashford Works).
T&RW	—	The Tramway and Railway World.
TMS	—	The Tramway Museum Society.
UDC	—	Urban District Council.
UEC	—	United Electric Car Co Ltd, Preston.
Walker	—	The Walker Electric Company, Cleveland, USA.
Westinghouse	—	Westinghouse Electric Co Ltd, Trafford Park, Manchester.

The Electric Railway & Tramway Carriage Works Ltd (renamed United Electric Car Company Ltd from 25 September 1905) was a subsidiary of Dick, Kerr & Co Ltd, which merged with other electrical companies on 14 December 1918 to form the English Electric Co Ltd.

Acknowledgments and Sources

This book is an abridged version of a two-volume hardback, *The Tramways of Kent,* published jointly by the Light Railway Transport League and the Tramway and Light Railway Society in 1971-5 under the editorship of Geoffrey E. Baddeley, and uses many of the same illustrations. The material on Bexley, Erith and Dartford is abridged from an earlier book, *The Tramways of Woolwich and South-East London,* issued by the same publishers in 1963. The three books were written under the noms-de-plume of 'Invicta' and 'Southeastern' by a panel of authors comprising F. Merton Atkins, G. E. Baddeley, A. W. Bond, R. Brimblecombe, R. J. Durrant, R. Elliott, A. Graham, A. A. Jackson, A. W. McCall, J. H. Price, D. Scotney, C. G. Stevens and D. W. Willoughby. Some portions (notably on Erith, by A. A. Jackson) had appeared previously in *Tramway Review,* and the history of Dover Tramways had been chronicled previously by J. V. Horn in his 1955 book *Dover Corporation Tramways, 1897-1936.*

We have taken the opportunity to check our previous work against that of more recent researchers in the same field, notably the two recent books by Brian Hart on the Folkestone cliff lifts and the Hythe and Sandgate horse tramway. The fleet lists on pages 44 to 48 have been compiled by J. H. Price, with the help of G. E. Baddeley, F. P. Groves, E. R. Oakley and A. G. Wells. A. A. Jackson and G. E. Baddeley supplied entries for the Bibliography.

We have repeated the best of the photographs from the previous three books, including some by the late Dr. Hugh Nicol, and record our thanks to the photographers and copyright holders, including the Science Museum for those taken by the late Dr. H. A. Whitcombe. Photographs newly added include some by the late G. N. Southerden, not previously available, and some commercial view postcards from the collection of J. H. Price. The map of the River Hospitals Tramway was traced by F. Merton Atkins, and the other maps were drawn by G. E. Baddeley (Bexley and Dartford), E. Beddard (Folkestone, Sandgate, Thanet), J. C. Gillham (Dover and Erith) and D. W. Willoughby (Chatham, Gravesend, Maidstone, Sheerness and the map of Kent). Photographs marked TMS are reproduced by permission of the Tramway Museum Society, from the R. B. Parr collection.

Periodicals consulted have included *Modern Tramway, Tramway Review, The Light Railway and Tramway Journal, The Tramway & Railway World, The Electrical Review* and the *BET Gazette*. Other sources are listed in the Bibliography.

Further books in this series will include one on the tramways of West Yorkshire and one on South Wales, and we shall be glad to hear from any reader with detailed knowledge of the pre-1928 trailer cars of the Swansea & Mumbles Railway.

Bibliography

General

Great British Tramway Networks, by W. H. Bett and J. C. Gillham (Light Railway Transport League, fourth edition, 1962).

Raworth's Regenerative Demi-Cars, by I. A. Yearsley (in *Tramway Review* 76 to 78, 1973/4).

Tramways Remembered — South and South East England, by L. Oppitz (Countryside Books, Newbury, 1988).

Bexley, Erith and Dartford

The Tramways of Woolwich and South East London, by 'Southeastern' (Light Railway Transport League and Tramway & Light Railway Society, 1963). The present book incorporates material from this work.

London County Council Tramways, by E. R. Oakley, Volume I (South London). London Tramways History Group, 1989.

Modern Tramway (Information Bureau), March 1947.

The Erith Urban District Council Tramways, by A. A. Jackson (in *Tramway Review* 22/23, 1957).

London's Last Horse Tramway, by J. H. Price (in *The Journal of Transport History*, May 1962).

Erith's Hire and Purchase of Trams, 1915-18, by G. W. Morant (in *Tramway Review* 132, 1987).

A more detailed bibliography will be found in Appendix 2 of *The Tramways of Woolwich and South East London*.

Gravesend

The Tramways of Kent — Volume One, West Kent, by 'Invicta' (Light Railway Transport League and Tramway & Light Railway Society, 1971).

Tramways in Gravesend and Northfleet, by Eric Fayne (in *Trams* Nos. 2 and 3, TMS, 1961).

Article in *The Engineer,* 15 March 1889, and *Illustrated London News,* 6 April 1889.

Article in *The BET Gazette,* March 1903.

Traction Without Parallel, by A. W. Bond (in *Modern Tramway,* February 1972).

Road Transport in Gravesend, by J. F. Parke (Omnibus Society, January 1943).

Medway Towns

The Tramways of Kent — Volume One, West Kent, by 'Invicta' (Light Railway Transport League and Tramway & Light Railway Society, 1971). The present book incorporates material from this work.

Tramways of the Medway Towns, by Eric Fayne (in *Trams* No. 19, October 1965).

Chatham and District, by L. Heath (unpublished paper, LRTL London Area, 10 March 1971).

The Chatham Accident, 1902, by M. J. O'Connor (in *Tramway Review* No. 2, 1950).

The Maidstone Trolleybus, by D. J. S. Scotney (National Trolleybus Association, 1972).

A Note on the Sheerness Tramways, by J. T. Smith and H. V. Jinks (in *Tramway Review* 29, 1961).

Sheerness correspondence in *Buses Illustrated,* issues 2, 10 and 11.

Catalogue issued by Siemens-Schuckert-Werke, Berlin, 1903.

Article on Maidstone trolleybuses in *Tramway & Railway World,* 12 July 1928.

Maidstone Corporation Transport (in *Modern Transport,* 23 July 1938).

Herne Bay

The Tramways of Kent — Volume Two, East Kent, by 'Invicta' (Light Railway Transport League and Tramway & Light Railway Society, 1975).

Herne Bay Pier — Three Tramways and a Mystery, by A. W. Bond (in *Modern Tramway,* April 1968).

Tramway and Railway World, 10 March 1910.

Correspondence in *Tramway Review* Nos. 140, 141 and 142; 1989/90.

Article on proposed (1901) tramway Whitstable-Herne Bay-Canterbury in *Chatham Observer,* 28 December 1956.

East Kent

The Tramways of Kent, Volume Two, East Kent, by 'Invicta' (Light Railway Transport League and Tramway & Light Railway Society, 1975). The present book incorporates material from this work.

Dover Corporation Tramways, 1897-1936, by J. V. Horn (Light Railway Transport League, 1955).

Articles on Dover in *Street Railway Journal,* June 1898 and in *Tramway and Railway World,* October 1897, May 1911 and August 1914.